MAGNIFICENT
M·A·P·L·E

by Marilee Robin Burton
illustrated by Cathy Diefendorf

MODERN CURRICULUM PRESS
Pearson Learning Group

I woke up early this morning and saw that the frost on the window had melted. The sky was blue and rays of sunshine were teasing me out of bed. My brother Jeff was already up and was first to notice the icicles dripping from the eaves of the roof outside our bedroom. It was the third day in a row we had awakened to a sunny sky.

"Time to start the maple run!" Jeff shouted. Then he hurried downstairs to tell Mom and Dad.

Every year, just about this time, Jeff and I help our parents make maple syrup from the sap of our sugar maple trees. Our family has a small grove of sugar maples called a sugarbush.

A maple grove is called a sugarbush because the most wonderful, sweet maple syrup comes from sugar maples. It's such hard work making the syrup that we sometimes feel exhausted and distressed. But in the end, it's all worth it!

We remove the sap by inserting tap-spouts in the trees. The sap then drips through the taps out of the tree and into buckets. That's called tapping the trees. This year I'll hammer the small metal taps into the trees. First Dad will drill holes an inch or two into the trunks. Then I'll hammer taps in each hole. Jeff will put the buckets over the taps to collect sap as it drips out. Once Jeff and I tried to count how many drips dripped out in a minute but we kept losing track. It was slow! Dad says there are about three hundred drips in an hour.

It will take Mom, Dad, Jeff, and me a couple of days to tap the trees in our sugarbush. We all work together. We can only tap trees when the sap is running, and that happens only for a short time in early spring when the days first start to get warm. The trees have been storing sap all winter underground in their roots. When the weather warms they start to send it up to the branches to help grow new leaves. But in the first days of spring it's still cold at night. If the temperature drops below freezing, the sap goes right back down to the roots. This up and down sap time is called the "run." It's the time to tap a tree. There's a short up and down time in fall too, but the sap from a fall run is not sweet.

Jeff and I have been getting up early all week and looking out the window to check the weather. You never know exactly when the run will start. Last year it was early, this year it's late. Watching for the right time is like playing a hide-and-seek game. You need a few warm days and cold nights in a row to make sure the sap is running.

Syrup season is short. The run lasts as long as there are warm days and cold nights. When it's warm all the time, the sap stops going up and down. It just goes up. The trees start to bud and then the new leaves need all the sap to help them grow. The best time for tapping the tree is over.

But now the best time for tapping is beginning. Today we'll go out and start to put taps in all the maple trees. Later on we'll filter the sap through a cloth. That will help us remove bits of bark and leaves.

It will take all day today and all day tomorrow to tap every maple in our sugarbush. Then Jeff, Mom, Dad, and I will start checking the buckets. A bucket fills up with sap in about a day. We get about ten gallons of sap in all from each taphole. That sounds like a lot, but it's really not. The sap gets boiled down to make syrup. After it's boiled, ten gallons of sap only makes one quart of syrup.

It takes an awful lot of sap to make a little syrup, so it's a good thing that trees make ample amounts of it! They make gallons and gallons of sap. They make much more than we use. We really only take a small portion, leaving most of the tree's sap for the tree. The tree uses it to grow healthy and strong. (And we sure want a sugarbush full of strong and healthy trees!)

When people made maple syrup a long time ago, they didn't always take good care of the trees. Instead of drilling small holes, they'd make big gashes with axes. The gashes really injured and distressed the trees. Those poor sugar maples weren't able to heal or recover. Insects would attack them, or they'd get diseased and die.

Now, people are more careful. We make small holes, and at the end of the run we take the taps out. The trees are able to heal over the small holes quickly. Their recovery is fast. If you walk through the sugarbush, you can see where the old tap holes were. You'll see bark scars in their place on the tree trunks.

Starting tomorrow, Jeff and I will make the rounds to search for full buckets. (And we'll taste the sap in some of the buckets along the way. It's sweet and good.) Full buckets get emptied into gathering buckets and then they go back on the tree for more sap. Gathering buckets get emptied into a gathering tank. The gathering tank is huge—it holds 128 gallons of sap! That's too big for anybody to carry.

Sadie and Bruno pull the gathering tank. They are our horses. We set the gathering tank on a wooden sleigh. The sleigh gets hitched to Sadie and Bruno. Then they drag it to the storage tank behind the sugarhouse. That's a small building in the middle of the sugarbush where we boil the sap into syrup.

Since it takes so much sap to make just a little syrup, we gather all the sap first before we start cooking it. Cooking takes a long time. It goes on all day and long into the night. We just have sandwiches for dinner on those nights because everybody's busy working. But it still feels like a holiday. The room gets steamy and smells sweet. Jeff and I get to stay up later than usual and all our neighbors stop by to visit. Mom makes tea with hot sap for everyone.

   Jeff's favorite part of the maple run is making the rounds and checking for full buckets. He likes running through the woods (or going through on skis if it's snowy) and tasting fresh sap straight from the buckets! I like that part too. But I think the most exciting part is when the sap is cooking. Dad stokes the fire. Jeff brings in wood. I help Mom skim the foam off the sap while it cooks.

Dad's job is hard because he has to keep wood burning all the time in the firebox under the evaporator. The evaporator is a giant stove with big shallow pans. When the sap cooks in the shallow pans on the stove, the water in it evaporates. Sap is mostly water. When the water evaporates, what's left behind is the sweet syrup! So sap gets cooked and cooked and cooked and cooked. It has to cook up to fifteen hours before it's ready. Jeff helps Dad by handing him wood for the fire.

When sap cooks, it bubbles into a foamy top that's called sugar-sand. It's kind of a gritty mineral deposit that bubbles up. Sugar-sand can also have dirt or bark pieces in it. We have to skim it off so the syrup will be clear and free of impurities. We have to be very careful of the hot sap, though, because hot sap is no fun if it drips on you.

All of the jobs are important. But sometimes it seems as if the most important one is at the very end— watching for the signs that the sap is turning to syrup.

And that job is up to everyone. We have a thermometer to test the temperature of the sap. Sap turns to syrup about 219°F, seven degrees above boiling. If it goes above that it will burn. It can even explode! But before the temperature rises, the sap turns a dark brown. The foam bubbles look different too. And the sap drips off the ladles in sheets or aprons instead of in little drips. "We have aprons!" someone will yell. Then quickly we check the thermometer. We check again, watching intently, waiting for exactly the right temperature. It happens fast.

"Syrup's ready!" someone will yell, and we'll all cheer loudly. The new syrup gets poured out of the evaporator into a big bucket. Dad will test it with a tool called a *hydrometer* (hy-DROM-iter) to make sure it's just the right density.

A gallon of syrup needs to weigh eleven pounds for it to taste and keep best. Then comes the final test. Dad pours out small cups of syrup and puts them on the shelf to cool. These are tasting cups. The final test is the taste test! The syrup will cool and then Dad will hand Jeff and me the small cups. We'll each take a sip . . . Mmmmm!!!

There's still a little more to do before we're all finished, though. The syrup still has to be poured through more filters. This is to make sure it's really clear and pure when it's finally ready. And it still has to be graded too. Mom will pour a little bit of the finished syrup into a small glass jar. She'll compare the color of the new syrup to bottles of syrup in a tester. She'll check to see whether it matches the light, medium, or dark color. Each color has a label called a *grade*. Syrup can be labeled *fancy*, *grade A*, or *grade B*.

We'll have pancakes and syrup as soon as the first syrup is ready. We'll have a huge pancake breakfast the very next morning. Jeff says that's the best part of syrup-making. I still say the best part comes with the first snow after the syrup is finished. Then Mom will boil up some of the new syrup to take outside. Jeff and I will make mounds of fresh newly fallen snow and pour hot syrup onto them. It cools right away and turns into taffy-like candy. We call it "sugar-in-the-snow." It's the best. It's delicious. It's magnificent.

Oh. There's Mom calling now. Time to start this year's run. There's lots of work to do, first, but it won't be long before I can say "Sugar-in-the-snow, here I come!"